Let's Hide from Mom
Copyright © 2024 by Parimalasri Docktor

All rights reserved. No part of this publication may be reproduced, distributed, or transmitted in any form or by any means, including photocopying, recording, or other electronic or mechanical methods, without the prior written permission of the author, except in the case of brief quotations embodied in critical reviews and certain other non-commercial uses permitted by copyright law.

Tellwell Talent
www.tellwell.ca

ISBN
978-1-77941-737-4 (Hardcover)
978-1-77941-736-7 (Paperback)
978-1-77941-738-1 (eBook)

As usual, I had difficulty going to sleep.

Let's Hide from Mom
I'm Not Sleepy Yet!

Written & Illustrated

By

Parimalasri Docktor

Krishna and I go to bed
on a heated mat.

Mom and Dad always cover us
with a soft mat or sometimes
a blankie to keep us protected
from cold and light at night.

Krishna said, "Radha, Mom is coming to tuck us in bed."

I said to him, "Let's hide from Mom- I am not sleepy yet."

As I was crawling to hide under the stool,

I saw Krishna climb the bridge.

I yelled, "Krishna, NOOO ... Mom can easily see you on the bridge. Go under the bridge."

Thud, thud, thud! Krishna came rolling down the bridge and fell on his back. I rushed to help Krishna flip back over.

I told him that we need to be quiet. I said to Krishna, "Let's hide in between our toys. Mom won't find us there."

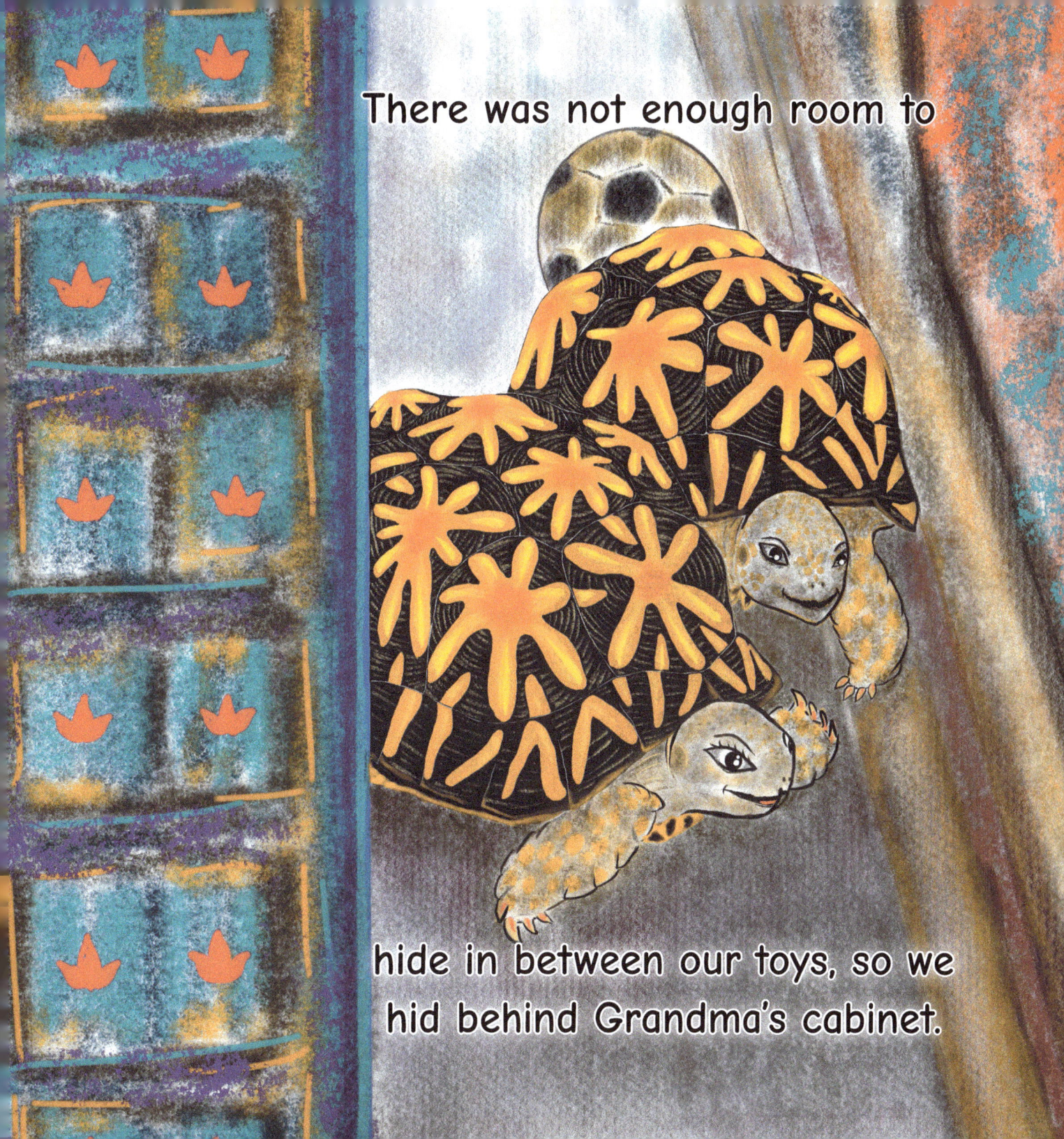
There was not enough room to hide in between our toys, so we hid behind Grandma's cabinet.

Mom called out, "Krishna, Radha, I hear you behind the cabinet."

Krishna and I decided to hide in Tank and Chili's cave, since Mom wouldn't look for us there.

Mom said, "I am turning out the lights. It is time for both of you to go to bed," and she closed the door on us!

We were not afraid of the dark. Mom wanted us to go to bed, but I was not sleepy yet.

Krishna said, "Radha, I am very sleepy. Try to go to sleep. You don't want Mom to take you to the vet for your sleeping disorder, do you?

Can we continue finding hiding places tomorrow?"

It's dark now. Dad is asleep. Mom is working and won't come out. Krishna is in bed. I am going to calm myself down.

 I will meditate like Mom to relax and go to sleep.

I will communicate silently through my heart in meditation with my mom so I can go to sleep.

Mom will tuck me in bed
when she sees me sleeping
outside the closed door.

Goodnight, everyone!

♥ Game 1. Let's play scavenger hunt in my playground.

Please find one of each:

Please find three of each:

Please find four different types of birds.

Please find six butterflies.

Please find 24 Indian Star tortoises.

♥ Game 2: Find just one bumble bee.

The End

www.ingramcontent.com/pod-product-compliance
Lightning Source LLC
LaVergne TN
LVHW072053060526
838200LV00061B/4725